FOR THE CHORUS

KEIRAN GODDARD

FOR THE CHORUS

EYEWEAR PUBLISHING

First published in 2014
by Eyewear Publishing Ltd
74 Leith Mansions, Grantully Road
London W9 1LJ
United Kingdom

Typeset with graphic design by Edwin Smet
Author photograph Benjamin Youd
Printed in England by TJ International Ltd, Padstow, Cornwall

ISBN 978-1-908998-32-3

WWW.EYEWEARPUBLISHING.COM

For Olivia

Keiran Goddard
was born and raised in Shard End,
Birmingham and educated at Oxford. His
work has previously been published in a number
of magazines and anthologies and his first
pamphlet, *Strings*, came out in 2013 from
Antler Press. This is his debut collection. He has
worked as a journalist and editor and in higher
education. He now works in the third sector,
is a poetry editor for The Squawk Back
and is undertaking a research project
on contemporary poetics. His other
interests include wine, whisky, books,
music and invective.

Table of Contents

Easy, easy Mr. Bones. I is on your side...
'Dream Song 36', John Berryman

The Soloist

The songs we liked
were the vanishing type,
simple enough to sing while we drank.
Nursery rhymes
about rivers and stones,
about wives, ghosts and fishermen in mourning.
You dutifully stood with us
at last orders,
a red ribbon pinned to your coat,
its gesture of charity
betraying you
as someone who wished for the novelties of war.

As you left
to return to your family,
I noticed your skin
was still brown from the summer.
Without you, amongst this sulphur
of cheap wine and withered lemon,
we were made to feel like rain
slowly darkening the edges of cardboard.
But dreaming to some purpose,
we regrouped, drew closer,
filled the gap
and balled our fists for the chorus.

Nape

What an utter anglepoise lamp of a neck you have,
you disconcertingly accurate thrower of light
on to the busted hunch of my bedroom furniture.

You have cast the ties looped on the back of my chair
as a festival plant, a waterfall of wax tongues
drooping from a branch above the city square.

Lit my jacket as two folded ravens
that have set their feathers and settled
for the night at the foot of the bed.

In the illuminated shrag of the floorboard
I am made beachcomber, botanist,
someone concerned with forestry.

I am struck, collecting twigs and etching
a comedian's circle around our feet.
I press a splintered finger against

the buttonhole of a bird's chest,
and edge myself quietly towards the light.

All Saints Church

That afternoon yawned open like toy scissors:
slack-jawed, blunt, and pointless.
In front of the pulpit a man played horsehair,
his right hand brittle and prone like a scorpion tail
while his elbow swung like a desperate shopper.

Our smiles were rows of cheap paper lanterns
flickering bright as chipped elephant bones,
excavated, tippexed clean, and sold in street markets.
Later we danced, moving as easily
as the breeze moves a dismembered elk.

You were missing until the morning,
discovered asleep and swaddled in tablecloth.
Your smile had altered from the night before,
now a keyboard of fragile ivory
crumbling at the thud of a clod-handed pianist

as he shattered his way through a prelude,
where, by necessity, no note was ever repeated.

Mantle

Sour wine, drunk
from the broiled skin
at the base of your neck:
tasting of warm cherries
then razor wire gnarled
into the shape of a feather.

Your name, scratched
in the orange dust
of an old house brick:
fingers worked raw
then a pulsing throat
as it slugs down the grit.

Stone moon, chanting
its endless psalm
of stillborn light:
I will never wax
I will never wane
I will steadily root out your every regret.

Playground Stuff

The last time you wrote me I didn't reply;
it was a postcard from Wales with a picture of boats.
Might have been from someone else entirely
but there is something about your 'Os'.
Always the same aberration;
a bald child with a bumped head
dropped in the course of some over the top swinging.

The Toast

He drank meltwater for thirst
served in a hackled wine glass.
It had oceaned in overnight
after the wound of song
he'd been flinging at ice
had finally begun to bear heat.

Hinging his arm he drank,
lukewarm and seal-grey waves.
To wasting another year on pleasure alone.
The words lodged in the root of his tongue,
squalled up its mizzenmast
then billowed his lips like a hymn.

He sang them louder as the years went on,
digging out a different throat,
as note by note
he matched the wrench
of time's ungainly
boneward grope.

Full Mouth

The imbalance of all this,
hanging cold around the words, *Dear Friend;*
your quiet sounds seem to address the dead,
I would have liked to talk to you more about the moon,
whose colour you confuse, from painful white, to painful red.

And the result,
sharing a bag of yellow plums on the late summer streets of a city,
stumbling dumb over the connection between
their yellow skin in brown paper,
and the stars' blank shine in this blind, ugly shuffle.

Two painters maybe, or one astronomer and a prophet,
but not two idiots, falling off a rope and smiling
and eating plums, and falling off a rope, and smiling.
I used to be able to reassure you with my words,
full mouth, Dear Friend, full mouth.

December 31, 2001

We all agreed on no honours and no decorations,
just a small gathering
to be held in the cemetery
that nestled its cheer against the tower blocks.

The pictures we took that night were guileless and affected;
I was wearing a slug of navvy rope as a belt,
hoping my face grease might seem heroic
if I mumbled enough things about the human spirit.

I was willing to spend the entire evening
shepherding the hairs on the slopes of her forearm
but, restless, she upped herself to dance
with the charitable wheeze of an old accordion.

Her expansion administered the sort of grief
that my teenage self was eager to blindfold and bolt down,
happy to invent the thrumming of tree bark
or an interest in the probable symbolism of a belfry.

We did stumble out of that year eventually
but only after I'd taken a clumsy detour down the seam of her dress,
stood guard over my ears for fear of rebuke,
then mumbled something true about the human spirit.

Pestle and Bowl

You, friend, are discord made dance,
you have come grappling your fortune in a pestle and bowl.
You have sat chiselling red rust from your bathtub,
hurdling your trenches with a lopsided skitter
and gently shambling a path toward refuge.

You have learnt that you cannot outpace a morning's shudder,
that you cannot illuminate a home with some candlesticks and a
          cook's match.
That although you can chide two flames into backlighting a life,
the gods are not flattered by prayers you don't mean.

You, friend, are the only man that I can imagine using the word *yell,*
the only man who, when faced with an entire ocean of flowers,
          would begin
an inner calculation designed to seek their exact number.
You are the only man I can picture *interrogating* an overcoat.

I have seen your tongue dither to reveal its larger truths,
drawing two thighs as slick dolphins arching out of a sea of blue dress.
Seen you begin your day's movements with a brutal, austere jolt
before swaying into life with the indeterminate sprig of something livi

There were times, when sick and hopeless as a fringe hacked too short,
I sought you as a drunk seeks the welcoming cold of the tiles.
In response you rounded up a mountain range and marked me out a pe
          to live on;
you, friend, are the very gentlest of horizons.

Days I have listened as you sang through a carnival of hourglass
reminding me again how your sound was always elegant and
gift-giving.
Days I have held you,
mustering the entire force of my will not to cry,
You, friend: never die, never die, never die.

Porcine

You swiftly traded the vagueness of sarcasm for the precision of insult;
you will lose me because you are an utterly disobedient lover,
because your insistent ransackery makes me feel dirty
and what you think of as charm has the ring of noxious smut.

I had said you were a fountain of fragrant vulgarities,
that your glamorous fasting had left you ugly about the eyes;
it prompted a river of mad, bare decreeing on the subject of my idiocy,
a charge of pig-headedness fierce enough to turn me porcine.

You will lose me because you drink wine from a bowl, you pig-head,
because it is like living with the ghost of a failed comedian,
because my heart only ever leaps with the stiffness
of a woman with two fractured kneecaps.

Mustering my protest I declare your lust the cut-out-and-keep kind,
the type I laminate to ward off the itch of hours in an office chair
and that if you leave I will certainly die a pauper,
or some mid-Atlantic panhandler of love songs.

Emeralds

Before the time came
for your ineffectual thinking
about legends and horsemen and emeralds,
you had prided yourself on tasting only of lemons,
and of wearing a scarf with more skill than your friends.
You had careered through wheat
with a boy of your choosing
a tangle of calves and a meeting of mouths,
and he remembers your legs had the power to tinder
his clinical voice into honourable sounds.

Rook

Upending your torch,
you swung an arc of light over the playground
and began to talk about invocation.
It started with you asking the darkness to justify itself,
and ended in a murmur of martyrs, crowns and the pity of names.

With a new-found shamanism you told me
that I would live my life in the shadow
of a pithy, black rook, offering me guidance
only when I learnt the divine power of his economy.

Pressing your tongue against the mud
you professed the endless majesty of renunciation
and asked me what I was willing to forsake,
all the time your voice ringing:

with a thudding, desolate gospel,
with the muted sound of a child
as it drops to its knees in a sandbox.

Harpoon

Tell me the truth about imminent disasters,
of chalky lips smoke-blowing grim arias
and hum me the shape of your blaze.
Don't shout it, but tell me how you manage
to never get washed up on sand shelves
when in reality you are not cut out for a life at sea.

Though I once dreamt of you, with the head of a fish,
and your fish eyes looked desperate,
and I cried a small Arabian sea in response,
(which you lived in without giving thanks)
I stand by my statement,
you seem ill-equipped for a life at sea.

I sought you there by holding my breath
and the canny use of specialist lanterns.
I followed you there with a diamond
and another present undisclosed.
Swimming downwards I had the poise of a whale
and hope burst in my blood like dangerous air.

I found the following things:
three dead bodies, shabbily dressed, five fish, heads intact,
an eternity of water, a mixture of nothing, with blue, with green,
(you must have been there somewhere)
but I was dragged upward like a graceless harpoon,
rusted in a factory before it ever met the sea.

Ledger

You accused the court of complacency,
assured them that, in your case,
you really were incandescent with rage.

That yes, you knew that people said incandescent
when they really meant quite angry
but that you had gone home and read by the light of your fury.

That you had birthed the true language of frustration,
of the frozen train track in the middle of spring
or a fireblast of soup edging the lip of a bowl.

I am not above a fracas, or an affray, you warned,
my anger has been known to blur a wedding photograph.
Please be sure to note that in your ledgers.

Windowsill

What miracles you pray for –
a future of stillness
in the shadow of this hanging fire.

Where you can dream shades of nature
that live between blue and black,
where from a market near your home
you can buy stone the colour of your body's ocean,
dress yourself in the green
you imagine the Pacific to be
and hope a life of submersion will bring forth new mercy.

Where you can swallow water
so a coughing child might begin to live,
until it starves in your plum-raw stomach
from a diet of no air. Where you will long to bury it,
as you have always buried cuttings from your past,
driven by the hope of growing
a future that is more tender.

Where you can disentangle your body
from your fear of the world,
as it peels back impropriety
and stands unclothed in its beauty and its dread,
where you can always be moved
by your awful unknotting
and the guttural fanfare when you are properly touched.

Jewel

I wrote you a note on a betting slip:
the jewel that you've lost
is the colour of nothing
but distance shorn of direction.

It was something to remedy
the cavity of your middle,
a new language
that spoke only of survival.

You said it made you burnish
though the only heat you knew
was paper being spat from flames
like black butterflies.

Turning to watch the sky
as it blanked and paled overhead,
there was no dusk to speak of,
just the slow removal of blue.

Collard Greens

When it came, it came trilling off her bottom lip:
this evening is taking on the taste of collard greens.
It landed like a dented tenor bell,
dancing a flat echo along the bar.

Against this trench of shadow
we saw the softened edge of a pear tree,
uncoarsened by the weight
of heavy rain slouching at its leaves.

*You seek beauty like those who require spectacles
but prefer the thumbed smudge of a jawline,* she explained.
Yet I can only hold her with the clumsy lattice of pillow on pillow
or as a small boy might an axe, or a large shovel.

I am made inexpert, proud.

Hero's Welcome

In the beginning
the rain shatters the wells,
turns the field
to lurid marsh, to an ocean
unlit and vast enough
to roar out demands.

We prepare to fight, shape
ourselves as soap arcs
against wet bone,
burn each of our boats
and later return, sheepish,
in our still-burning boats.

Love Letter

Slattern, hallower,
I have an answer to your silence,
I will scream the words to 'Danny Boy'
into your waiting lap

Slattern, hallower
I will rise from this chair
to make speeches about a war
that I never lived through

Slattern, hallower,
I will take care of my skin,
so as to offer the comfort
of a texture you know

Slattern, hallower,
I will divide post-piss mirror time
equally between
shame, pride and boredom

Slattern, hallower
I will follow your rambles,
wade in the stiff phlegm of the dead
just to locate your point

Slattern, hallower
I will always imagine a landscape at your back
bigger than this bar wall
Yours, sincerely, the Shipwrecker's Arms.

Prodigal

Seeking a small distraction
I watched your son muster
a tremor of bored energy
and snap off a vine in his fist.

Like a monarch concerned
with the saga of ritual feast
he coiled it on his hairline
and stayed deaf to the chant of his name.

Until, afire with a plan,
he wrapped up his wrists
in the manacle plants
before raising his arms with a smile.

Blue Room

Now I know how I sought you –
in my blindness I swung skyward,
searching for the sound of a hungry, songless gull,
finding only the soft upward crane of your neck,

the distant dart of your tears
running back into your eyes,
sieve-filling your skull,
signalling the start of your drowning,

imagined you on coasts,
telling secrets to dead shells,
watching others throw pebbles against cliffs,
and silently deciding

to throw your weakening body instead.
Then, at last, years later,
your blue room,
bathed in the dullest of sea light.

Mermaid Quay

There was a bay that stayed open for drinkers,
for the steady clack of unclad women,
jarring out beats from the heels of their shoes.

In its undertone of shuffle,
you noted the moping potency of the boys,
and imagined their pockets jammed with receipts.

Wondered whether, at the end of an evening,
they tore them to bountiful tatters
and threw them to the wind like confetti.

We danced to a song we didn't know,
with the metric novelty of a watch
fastened for the night to the wrong person's wrist.

A slash of red wine in the corner of your mouth
struck me as hasty medicine,
slopped down your throat by a passing stranger.

As our bodies moved in an awkward canon,
I knew only the anatomy of gratitude
and sang an entire sky of it from my chest.

In the draught and the mist of that city's inletting,
in its nearest museum of wreck and of wreath,
I felt a seafarer's jeopardy at the thought of your leaving.

Steersmen

In the corner of our garden
was a sprung ribcage,
we placed a blue candle
inside of its maw,

we watched for hours,
on the trunk of a pear tree
we'd newly garrotted
for growing too tall.

We joked, *our animal lantern*
but had begun to believe
that if we kept it well lit
it would shield us from harm.

It bound us finally as steersmen,
each dreading
a wind cold enough
to put an end to its light.

Clot

It is not coldness that blisters this land white,
it is the brittle sun,
edging your legs apart
and pulling out clot.

Despite his stained teeth,
his thick blood,
you insist you wished him this way,
that you grew his name
under a swollen tongue.

In truth, he was unforeseen,
a timesick breech of a child,
who will end his days
broke-backed on your dinner table.

His hairless chest will breathe
a lump-heavy warning drone:
I create the air I need to exist,
who will hold you when my will ends?

Foresight

I saw you stalk a lake,
praying for wind
to come tipping at wildlife,

heard you laugh like a crank
as it forced over ducks
and sent them panicking upright,

watched you actually heckle the geese
hurry up and swim!
you slow geese bastards!

It was as sad and as pointless
as a person slowly
rising into parable.

Unclosed

You sit shallow and wait,
while the air around you is scream-full of miracle,
while the new dead reawaken
to dance you back to your door,
to mutter into your neck
the secret you had sewn yourself to keep,
every drop of blood that is drawn
will be repaid and reborn in the heat of the stars.

To suggest that everything real has a horizon,
that every measured march needs
a space left chiming for visions,
that all a looking glass will ever show you
is how sickness wishes you to look,
to ask why this photograph is so insistently silent,
why it allows no wind within its borders,
to offer *every day's most quiet need, by sun and candlelight.*

All this time you talk only of another country,
when so much of this world is unclosed.

Shoreline

At the last it came to very little,
all that mooning about on the marl of tarmac,
crunched under your heel like sugar
pressed against the face of a teaspoon.

With the air tricking over your ears
I had watched you jig along entire
cities of pavement, splinter the angry greenness of apple
into the muted glass of oncoming traffic,

stop to grind a broken pencil into the palm
of every tenth passer-by, insist when challenged
that a prophecy can only ever be felt to be true,
and throw a starling of smile to beg for their pardon.

That luggageless stride along the warp of dark alley
half-lacquered in waves of hasty gravel
lent your movement the grace of a saviour
stepping with ease from the sand to the salt.

Saul Bellow (1915-2005)

I heard of your death as my sister came bounding
with her genderless baby afloat in a cone.
I had hoped for your whisper of truth at the end,
not this worshipping life, forty-five per cent grown.

For a second the city felt windless,
so I filled it with the words that were closest to hand:
all these books and this music and this laughter,
a man just cannot be heard above the bird noise.

I was just discovering you when you left,
which ruined my dream of us, in matching felt hats,
two dapper but reluctant partygoers
always intent on getting things properly talked out.

Protracted

I wrote you for three straight days
and four nights, bent out of shape
and then I saw you, and it seemed
you were re-learning how to move,
like you once knew,
but someone took it while you slept.
You were making strange angles,
an amateur human, new to your craft.
You dared the world
to cast itself around you.
It refused.
And with no ceremony
to recall this,
I will lose it in time to the wind.

Hen and Chickens Public House

This year, intent on rest,
we bevelled out a thoroughly novice winter
by scraping an earring along a stick of old classroom chalk.
We could do better, I'd imagine, but we are
thick-eyed and carol-deaf from four hours of bad radio.

At night here, there are constellations of blackboard dust,
and we use them to plot out pretend maps of the north –
here are the valleys of the chartists, and the covens
and the handsome, guilty, animal poets
and their handsome, guilty, dead wives.

By morning, the dust has settled in the villages,
been trodden into a compact spine by ramblers in ugly trainers.
We wake later and shuffle up its notches, like pilgrims,
our destination, the Hen and Chickens Public House,
the type of building the English use to fall in love.

We leave half-cut, ringing from the tyranny of the jukebox,
eager to talk but remembering at the last moment that speaking now
or forever holding our peace is not an either/or choice.
And again you are filling my thoughts. And I am put in mind of music
or home, or any number of things that I am grateful exist.

Indoors

That winter there were more brambles
and us, indoors, trying not to scratch our hands.
Your duty to remain had bound you
to a form wrapped and ready for worship –
look at the wife in twine,
it is said she is riddled with echo.

But an age away, I am drifted in scarlet
reading your healing between the breaths
of tongue and the shiver of wound.
Godless in this split second back-peel of bandage,
I see the whiteness of healing
and am finally alive to the truth of rebirth.

Brink

And then came your fear
in half of the half-light:

the blank scream of water,
your wounds soon packed
in soil and in silt.

And then came your chaos,
the ache of bark against bare back:

the shadow of a god
sparking into life
and ghosting across your hips.

And then came your stillness,
the arch of branch under bird wing:

the flame of your next breath,
to be held, then released,
and then suddenly sealed in glass.

Ham Fist

It would be fitting to remember your sound
as the delicate whisper of calfskin on drumstick
and yet, when I play back the cassette,
it is just the hiss
of a ham-fisted opportunist
playing ham with his fist.

You make the sound of a rusty coin
echoing in the hollow gut of a charity bear,
of a hacking cough catching the lip of a beer bottle,
managing to flute out something rounder
before hitting the cold brown glass,
on the off beat. By chance.

His thick arms:

wield an ornamental coal shovel
he found rusting on a hearth
before the heat pricked
all bravery from his gesture,

a gap in his teeth is a firebreak
preventing his child's finger
running corner to corner
and forcing him to smile,

the ache of his gums
renders fruit a living friend
glimpsed in a tavern following
a destructive year of bubonic plague,

he daydreams of
unexpected nimble-fingered riggers
flecked with gunpowder arriving at points
of nautical peril with a convincing gait,

of crude hooks battered into salmon skulls
reduced to a complex stock
(he adds additional flavour notes
from the unused perfume of ladies)

of the child slipping its reins
running through his fingers like oil,
of approaching love with Zeno-skulk
never touching, always edging closer.

How I remember:

the white-water swell at her lip-join
the tender effort of sleep
ribboning from temple to chin

the rainstorm of silver
lying trapped under silk
and her body that asks for permission to break

the ink of her fingers
as they spread under street lamps
a shadow of branch I wrap round her wrist

and the endless will
of her dawn-light searching
for only the shapes that feel right in her fist.

Cliff Notes

Burnt Norton:
With your teeth in my shoulder the turn of the world span still.
Consider the shape of a space unmoving,
where there is only the dancing and time's own undoing.

Ariel:
Nothing moves here, in the black.
Except the blue,
eyes, your real eyes, are bowls of sad-soup.

To the Lighthouse:
There is room for one miracle every day,
so she strikes one match, every day,
there is too much night though, every day.

Ode to a Nightingale:
I listened darkly, lots of times,
until I learnt how to tell, upon waking,
what birds you had dreamt of.

Jude the Obscure:
If I never see you again, keep reading,
be kind to animals,
and never stop writing about being a bird.

Tat Men

Intimacy demanded we jaw about childhoods,
so I told you that in Birmingham we called them the *tat men,*
that they drove flatbed trucks piled with a shipwreck
of twisted bike frames and the undersides of washing machines.

That they would pay you a pound if you clambered the fence
to the birdless shrub of courtyard behind the flats,
that we carried anything metal we could manage
and wiped our arms on a rag so our moms wouldn't know.

You talked about dipping your hands in paint,
about only liking it when you could see each one of your digits,
about how the first time you saw a map, pinned to a classroom wall,
you thought its fingerless shapes were a failure of technique.

You laughed, not knowing that this vision of you had broken
something in me as a lake breaks under the first drop of rain,
that every morning after I would see the faint mark of rust,
left in the space where I last tilled your skin.

Bankroll

You ended a night's worth of card game
by tumbling the pack to the floor,
declared the end of festivities,
with the blunt inflection of a mob
watching a drunk highwayman
handle the loot of the poor.

Then gathered them up
with an emerald bend
flexed at the bulb of your knuckle,
clutched at forgiveness
in a fistful of suits,
and folded each wing you'd plucked from the swarm.

On Foot

That slow millennial walk, the one toward your magmatic blinding,
that was gentle wasn't it? and frightening.
I was then, and remain, unsure as to whether the trees stayed bare
or burst greener than ever the spring after you were born.
For you insist upon being of no nature and of no cause,
and of brutally objecting to the bulk of your own matter.

I remember you in evenings, pretending you were not leaving,
preparing to transform your inner world,
and failing,
all heart wail and wild, pointless force,
but finally lacking a steady enough hand
to hold and shape the raw clay of change.

And then nothing happened, or if it did I do not understand
           what it was,
something about you becoming an animal, of some sort,
and then becoming the ghost of an animal,
and then coming like a siege, of some kind, or another.
And then of me, cold in the dawn sun,
tracing the scratches on your back: the trail of comets
too distant to follow on foot.

Walk

In all of this walking we had managed
to gut out our days in darkness,
and begin the process
of repeating every gesture we had ever made.

We became four feet tolling
in every silent minute of the earth,
in every hour of it, and every week and month and life of it,
for all that it meant to us then.

And how many times we circled your street,
and how many times I didn't mention
the loops of black wire,
gripping like hands to the roof of your house.

I couldn't bear that you had spent
each night in that shape,
or that you'd noticed the wire before
but thought it looked like something else entirely.

When the exhaustion came, you slept,
and I watched your chest pulse like a dull glass bell.
I, meanwhile, kicked around in ashes and grief,
whispering that I have you, lying.

How else do I come to you now
apart from in dreams, a spark rushing upward
then falling back to the fire?
Breathe on this, sorrow this, see what happens when we walk.

Captain's Rest

As I stood, watching your spindled limbs
untie boat after boat from their moorings
I was lifted to a state of weakling's rapture.

With a smug destruction of old code,
I was keeping the secret of our river –
the long hidden knot we'd lodged in its bed.

I knew it would force every vessel
along a wracked and unexpected course;
grinding against the dry rivets of the settlement.

Mindless and altered by daylight
I sank pintfuls of salty words
and beamed as the visible telling unfolded.

You, holding splinters of jutted wood
at the end of their featureless climb –
beginning to grapple with the privacies of grief.

The sun, shuttering up brickwork,
leaving our port in shadow, untended,
in the needless crossfire of starlight on water.

And the Dreamers

The deaf years
ended with a thick, forgotten
stone of a song

rising, uninvited
from the dry earth
we'd packed around our lungs.

It demanded we anchor
it neck deep and near
to rivers or roads

so it could sense
escape and braid
its hopes in grass and in vine.

Later, we all lived
in a thunder of sound
while that stone drank

only from wounds
and heard only the dry
notes of weightless air.

We hold it again now,
as seven brothers
might carry the eighth

or seven dented
church bells might catch
new light as they move.

By each speaking
a version of prayer,
we gifted each other that stone

then gathered its truths
and returned to our home,
replanted its music where its music had grown.

Slapstick

A week ago you slipped on a dog,
stumbling head first into comedy,
a cymbal-crash of knee,
and the splinter of bone into thirty-eight pieces.

All thirty-eight were inside of you still,
not quick enough to escape,
to leave and forge new lives
in warmer climes than your knee could offer.

You wondered at the fate of them all,
as your knee sat wrapped
like a family secret in chip-shop paper
(that dad stuffed in his pocket before dishing up tea).

In time you forgot the thirty-seven strays,
they left, banded together, set off
for a dust bowl adventure and a widening sky
(only one remained, a pale admirer unafraid to be alone).

This one claimed he loved you, against your will.
You wished that he would leave: catch up with the rest,
form a new kneecap in yet-to-be-rained-on places,
or at least find some space going spare in a fish.

Strings

You were not born near enough to the water to know it,
but were close enough to feel its metal at weekends,
and on bruised evenings as you cliff-wound by car.
Those nights, asked to give yourself to the melody,
you gave precisely, but with a stark coast of inner division.

In time, the *détaché* you inhabited by rote
would come to govern more than just your hands,
as beat by beat, you undid your life in a rage of discords
(played with near-nimble wrenching of long-broken things,
from ten shrub-tree fingers on four gut-compass strings).

It is some other time now, and your breath roars
like a distant breaker on my neck.
The bedroom is lit by street lamps, a lifetime
of false twilights on sticks. You will wake soon,
and in minutes the house tap will flood between your fingers.

It is said that the sea gives a taste for adventure,
but when the waves hit you never did thirst to leave.
Instead, every tide dislodged something tiny,
creating the space that you needed
to make your music sadder still.

Fixed Price Menu

The morning splits into the thinnest of lines,
shanks through the window and hangs lazy on a fork-edge
and the rest is for when the rest has gone down.

The evening stutters over the browned serving spoon,
stops, apologises, then settles on a carrot,
and the rest is for when the rest has gone down.

Laced

You unwind a bruise of silk
from a tangle of underwear
and gather up its colour
against the bower of your back

Tell me it holds a ponytail
with more strength than a hairclip
these can take two thighs and a waist
or a wolf, or a bison, or a boar...

Then came our choice –
witter about lips and hands
and breasts, and bibles
and third-generation coffee

Or stagger like boxers, punch-drunk
into the very mind of God
and uncoil its knotted whorl
of lack mixed with hair mixed with lace.

In Time

after R.S Thomas

I sometimes wonder if I will lose you to time,
and then, in stillness, time itself answers me:
was it not in me that you found her?
was it not in me that she came to you?
was it not in me that you waited?
Forced to agree, I concede:
it was in time that I felt her hand move across my face,
it was in time that I understood,
that time will pass, and my face will cave,
that her eyes will open to the space
filled now by an old man,
trembling in love like a child.

Brother is Born
Proverbs 17:17

Map with brittle folds,
shot with sketches,
black circus wheeling through town
confessing every mark –
a cudgelled heap of supple hounds,
a felled ash tree,
a mouth gasping in solitary air.

Pill forced through foil bed,
ill-weathered stone
breaking the skin of water,
addressing the night in whisper –
if I am held,
I am significant,
I am lambent in moonlight.

Final pair on dance floor,
a grief seen in glances,
the edge of smile,
cracked like hot soil –
I am the frailty of charcoal,
held in a sculptor's rough hand,
I shiver like dust in the arc of a sunbeam.

Distant canticle,
friendship's steady foot-fall.
A hymn with the strength to rise to,
the sheer truth –
love's slow,
purposeful
healing of wounds.

Tambourine

Above all else, I am a man that dies,
though on reflection, I have also slept,
and I have felt a wall fall over,
and I have seen a black rock being kissed by birds,
or bitten, and I once heard a tambourine.
I know this because I still hear it,
it is in my memory when I walk.
Some nights, the clatter is unbearable,
I am shred cold by lightning
and wish music was something you could bury.
Enough of that though, to you for a time.
Although there is some sprawl between our bodies,
I can hear your breathless whine in the darkness,
can see that there are days
when your tongue is something dry you want to spit out.
I would gladly still kiss you,
catch the dust in my throat, ready for the singing.

Armistice

If you can stop your commanding of weather,
and stoically polish your own hunting horn,
if you can take all the sadness of losing,
then there is no real cause for the ending of war.

If you can pierce a man with a hairpin
and map battlefields using only your chalk,
if you can be storm displaced from a teacup,
then there is no real cause for the ending of war.

If you can be constantly resting your cases,
and steadily stringing your veins to the stars,
if you can be more than an urge to dismantle,
then there is no real cause for the end of our war.

Pastures

The morning had brought the haunting caution
of a harvest of crystal appearing while you slept.

It had shifted your leaving into a dance
of shimmered stooping through long grass
as the new snow powdered your shin bone.

In the incremental thickening of daylight,
you were still fleet, still wan, still phantom.

You passed the darkened hood of a blackbird,
and I imagined the sound of a cloistered bell,
tolling out the first lilt of winter.

The frosted lawn waltzed in response.
I felt your body in every blade of it.

The Engineer

As the last empire fell, your body still moved
with the quivering pomp of the emperor's band,
full and upstanding, until collapse came and shook you,
in an angleless swelter of brass and of sand.

I had watched as your hands stroked the back of old corsets,
and plucked out the bones like a fisherman's fly,
as you subtly edged out a break in the surface,
then showcased your version of life to the skies.

In striking your tune you played cartilage with matchstick,
your approximate anthem of homeland and ease,
before sliding the bone back inside of the rivets
that sat wanting on ribs and awaiting release.

It rang like a bird song on echoless beaches,
and I am lit like a lamp powered only by oil,
I am holding your wings in their floundering pieces
and I plant them with hope in the mouth of the soil.

Trappist

In a lifetime
unshrugged from the burden of prayer
he had torn at skies like a child
attacking the edges of gift wrap.
And yet, it is in dumb,
monastic silence
that he finds his gaze cleaved
to the equator of her eyeline.
To a face that holds the rumour of scarlet
like a bead of blood
washed pink
under the heavy throb of a distant river.

Not for Food that Spoils
John 6:27

Work has ended for the day
so I am now planning to ingest your teeth
by breaking the glass skin hung
over your mandible, your maxilla,
and your other bones, all close-knit and prim.

I will dig like a starving marshbird
beak-ing at the swag of your gum,
rooting out your decaying mouth,
hungry for brown chloride edges
and the memory of factories broiling out flame.

I will roll your rot against my tongue,
lick it white then set it to swim
in the dank acids of my stomach,
sure that this is a devout moment
and that gold wings will soon open inside me.

Marbles

It has happened –
we have finally begun to fear jokes.
Until now they have rung
like the sound of departing sirens,
reminding us that every corpse
unfurled from a carpet
is meant only for the floor
of another person's home.

Now they roll unwelcome
as scratched marbles
sat beneath a tide of tissue,
daring the bravest among us
to test glass against jawbone
to throw dwarf planets on lino
and risk the kind of black and white fall
we pretend to remember from childhood.

17:32

Somewhere between Euston and New Street
the year's rust blushed itself into our bones.
Steadily, from neck to ankle
we became frail copper piping
edging ourselves towards hazard,
spitting dumb threats at our furniture...
how do you fancy a future as driftwood?

Chasing the King of Hearts

In the silent hours,
reborn as a hunter
you spit four teeth
into your cupped hand.

They settle in the gutter
of your fingers –
the whitewashed skulls
of miniature birds.

You offer them as votives:
Dearest, do you remember these –
the first four buttons
you tore from my dress?

As battered tuning pegs:
Dearest, remember you yawed
each one in turn
until that song came right?

As the gravestones of others:
Dearest, remember that man in flames
with the sea at his back?
It is because of me that he lived.

Something Something Heath

It is not wine
that makes weak
hearts weaker

or a stitch
work loose
from a lifetime of wear

but the deaf
belief
that cadence

will flirt
with ruin
then resolve to land

that when
the final
bow is arced

you will
not hear
that you have wasted love.

Acknowledgements

Thanks go to the editors of *Warwick Review*, *Poetry Salzburg Review*, *Magma*, *The Rialto*, *Brautigan Free Press*, *Naked Lungs*, *Acumen*, *The Squawk Back*, *PEN*, *Mercy*, *Arvon* and *Antler Press* all of whom have previously published versions of the poems contained in this book. Thanks also to Todd Swift, Luke Kennard, Gillian Clarke, Carol Ann Duffy and Peter Robinson for their editorial input.

EYEWEAR PUBLISHING